Virtualization: A Manager's Guide

Virtualization: A Manager's Guide

Dan Kusnetzky

Beijing · Cambridge · Farnham · Köln · Sebastopol · Tokyo

Virtualization: A Manager's Guide
by Dan Kusnetzky

Published by O'Reilly Media, Inc., 1005 Gravenstein Highway North, Sebastopol, CA 95472.

O'Reilly books may be purchased for educational, business, or sales promotional use. Online editions are also available for most titles (*http://my.safaribooksonline.com*). For more information, contact our corporate/institutional sales department: (800) 998-9938 or *corporate@oreilly.com*.

Editor: Mike Hendrickson	**Cover Designer:** Karen Montgomery
Production Editor: Teresa Elsey	**Interior Designer:** David Futato
Proofreader: Teresa Elsey	**Illustrator:** Robert Romano

Printing History:

June 2011:	First Edition.

ISBN: 978-1-449-30645-8

[LSI]

1307548564

Table of Contents

Preface

About This Book

This book is intended to introduce managers or subject matter experts outside of information technology (IT) to the concepts behind virtualization technology, the different categories of virtualization, and how they are used. It is not meant to replace product documentation. It is not meant as a "how to" guide for IT analysts, developers, or administrators.

Conventions Used in This Book

The following typographical conventions are used in this book:

Italic
> Indicates new terms, URLs, email addresses, filenames, and file extensions.

`Constant width`
> Used for program listings, as well as within paragraphs to refer to program elements such as variable or function names, databases, data types, environment variables, statements, and keywords.

`Constant width bold`
> Shows commands or other text that should be typed literally by the user.

`Constant width italic`
> Shows text that should be replaced with user-supplied values or by values determined by context.

Using Code Examples

This book is here to help you get your job done. In general, you may use the code in this book in your programs and documentation. You do not need to contact us for permission unless you're reproducing a significant portion of the code. For example, writing a program that uses several chunks of code from this book does not require permission. Selling or distributing a CD-ROM of examples from O'Reilly books does require permission. Answering a question by citing this book and quoting example code does not require permission. Incorporating a significant amount of example code from this book into your product's documentation does require permission.

We appreciate, but do not require, attribution. An attribution usually includes the title, author, publisher, and ISBN. For example: "*Virtualization: A Manager's Guide* by Dan Kusnetzky (O'Reilly). Copyright 2011 Kusnetzky Group LLC, 978-1-449-30645-8."

If you feel your use of code examples falls outside fair use or the permission given above, feel free to contact us at *permissions@oreilly.com*.

Safari® Books Online

Safari Safari Books Online is an on-demand digital library that lets you easily search over 7,500 technology and creative reference books and videos to find the answers you need quickly.

With a subscription, you can read any page and watch any video from our library online. Read books on your cell phone and mobile devices. Access new titles before they are available for print, and get exclusive access to manuscripts in development and post feedback for the authors. Copy and paste code samples, organize your favorites, download chapters, bookmark key sections, create notes, print out pages, and benefit from tons of other time-saving features.

O'Reilly Media has uploaded this book to the Safari Books Online service. To have full digital access to this book and others on similar topics from O'Reilly and other publishers, sign up for free at *http://my.safaribooksonline.com*.

How to Contact Us

Please address comments and questions concerning this book to the publisher:

> O'Reilly Media, Inc.
> 1005 Gravenstein Highway North
> Sebastopol, CA 95472
> 800-998-9938 (in the United States or Canada)
> 707-829-0515 (international or local)
> 707-829-0104 (fax)

We have a web page for this book, where we list errata, examples, and any additional information. You can access this page at:

> *http://www.oreilly.com/catalog/0636920020417/*

To comment or ask technical questions about this book, send email to:

> *bookquestions@oreilly.com*

For more information about our books, courses, conferences, and news, see our website at *http://www.oreilly.com*.

Find us on Facebook: *http://facebook.com/oreilly*

Follow us on Twitter: *http://twitter.com/oreillymedia*

Watch us on YouTube: *http://www.youtube.com/oreillymedia*

CHAPTER 1

A Model of Virtualization

Model of Virtualization

Analysts often find that it is much easier to understand a complex environment if they build a reference model. The Kusnetzky Group Model of virtualization (Figure 1-1) is an example. Reference models must be comprehensive and the segments must be mutually exclusive to be really useful.

Over time, most of the functions that computers perform have in some way benefited from virtualization. It is important to note that some products incorporate features that straddle one or more layers of the model. Those products are typically assigned to the layer describing their most commonly used functions. As one would expect, industry and technological changes require that the model be revisited regularly to determine if previous categories should be merged into a single new category or deleted.

What Is Virtualization?

Virtualization is a way to abstract applications and their underlying components away from the hardware supporting them and present a logical or virtual view of these resources. This logical view may be strikingly different from the physical view. The goal of virtualization is usually one of the following: higher levels of performance, scalability, reliability/availability, agility, or to create a unified security and management domain.

This virtual view is constructed using excess processing power, memory, storage, or network bandwidth.

Virtualization can create the artificial view that many computers are a single computing resource or that a single machine is really many individual computers. It can make a single large storage resource appear to be many smaller ones or make many smaller storage devices appear to be a single device.

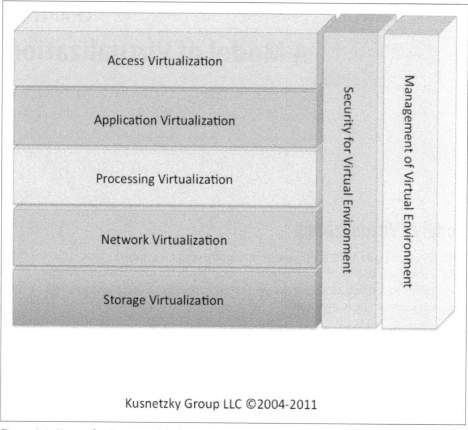

Figure 1-1. *Kusnetzky Group model of virtualization*

Layers of Virtualization at Work

There are many layers of technology that virtualize some portion of a computing environment. Let's look at each of them in turn.

Access virtualization

Hardware and software technology that allows nearly any device to access any application without either having to know too much about the other. The application sees a device it's used to working with. The device sees an application it knows how to display. In some cases, special-purpose hardware is used on each side of the network connection to increase performance, allow many users to share a single client system, or allow a single individual to see multiple displays.

See Chapter 2 for more information.

Application virtualization

Software technology allowing applications to run on many different operating systems and hardware platforms. This usually means that the application has been written to use an application framework. It also means that applications running on the same system that do not use this framework do not get the benefits of application virtualization. More advanced forms of this technology offer the ability to restart an application in case of a failure, start another instance of an application if the application is not meeting service-level objectives, or provide workload balancing among multiple instances of an application to achieve high levels of scalability. Some really sophisticated approaches to application virtualization can do this magical feat without requiring that the application be re-architected or rewritten using a special application framework.

See Chapter 3 for more information.

Processing virtualization

Hardware and software technology that hides physical hardware configuration from system services, operating systems, or applications. This type of virtualization technology can make one system appear to be many or many systems appear to be a single computing resource, to achieve goals ranging from raw performance, high levels of scalability, reliability/availability, agility, or consolidation of multiple environments into a single system.

See Chapter 4 for more information.

Network virtualization

Hardware and software technology that presents a view of the network that differs from the physical view. A personal computer, for example, may be allowed to "see" only systems it is allowed to access. Another common use is making multiple network links appear to be a single link. This approach makes it possible for the link to present higher levels of performance and reliability.

See Chapter 5 for more information.

Storage virtualization

Hardware and software technology that hides where storage systems are and what type of device is actually storing applications and data. This technology allows many systems to share the same storage devices without knowing that others are also accessing them. This technology also makes it possible to take a snapshot of a live system so that it can be backed up without hindering online or transactional applications.

See Chapter 6 for more information.

Security for virtual environments

Software technology that controls access to various elements in a virtual environment and prevents unauthorized or malicious use.

See Chapter 7 for more information.

Management for virtual environments

Software technology that makes it possible for multiple systems to be provisioned and managed as if they were a single computing resource.

See Chapter 8 for more information.

Each of these layers of virtualization will be examined in the following chapters.

Goals of Virtualization

Organizations are often seeking different things when using virtualization technology. An organization's virtualization goals might include the following:

- Allowing any network-enabled device to access any network-accessible application over any network, even if that application was never designed to work with that type of device
- Isolation of one workload or application from another to enhance security or manageability of the environment
- Isolation of an application from the operating system, allowing an application to continue to function even though it was designed for a different version of the operating system
- Isolation of an application from the operating system, allowing an application to function on a foreign operating system
- Increasing the number of people that an application can support, by allowing multiple instances to run on different machines simultaneously
- Decreasing the time it takes for an application to run, by segmenting either the data or the application itself and spreading the work over many systems
- Optimizing the use of a single system, allowing it to work harder and more intelligently (that is, reducing the amount of time the processor sits idle)
- Increasing the reliability or availability of an application or workload through redundancy (if any single component fails, this virtualization technology either moves the application to a surviving system or restarts a function on a surviving system)

The organization's choice of virtualization technology is dependent upon what it's trying to accomplish. While there are typically many ways to accomplish these goals, some goals direct organizations' decision-makers to select specific tools.

CHAPTER 2

Access Virtualization: Providing Universal Access

What Is Access Virtualization?

As we dive deeper into the model (see Figure 2-1), we start to understand how a virtual environment is created. Access virtualization hardware and software are designed to place access to applications and workloads in a virtual environment. The user interface, the business rules processing (the series of steps that make an application work), the data, and the storage management functions reside back in the network on a server. The server supporting this processing could be a Blade PC, a Blade Server, a virtual server, or a physical server. This technology allows "any place, any time, any device" computing.

As with other virtualization technologies, access virtualization has a long track record of success. The earliest forms of access virtualization were developed by mainframe suppliers, such as IBM, Burroughs (now part of Unisys), RCA, and others, to allow clusters of terminals to access applications running in the data center.

In 1983, the Massachusetts Institute of Technology (MIT) partnered with IBM and Digital Equipment Corporation (now part of HP) in the Athena Project. The goal was to create a campus-wide computing environment. One of the products of that collaboration was the X-Windows system. X-Windows, now available for UNIX, Linux, Windows, and many mainframe environments, is another early example of access virtualization.

Windows has been the center of intense development of access virtualization as well. Citrix, Microsoft, and the X-Windows community have been offering virtual access to Windows applications since the late 1980s.

Today, this type of virtualization is often used in conjunction with various forms of processing virtualization, which will be examined in Chapter 4. It is also an important component of desktop virtualization, virtual desktop infrastructure (VDI), and some

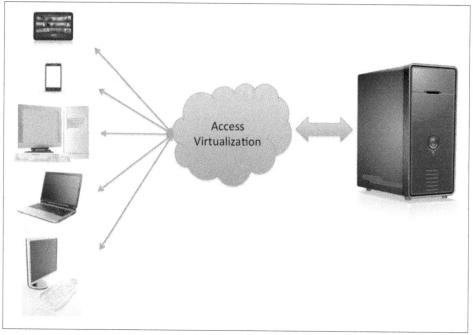

Figure 2-1. Access virtualization

forms of cloud computing, such as Software as a Service (SaaS). Desktop virtualization and VDI will be considered in Chapter 9.

What Does Access Virtualization Do?

As shown in Figure 2-2, access virtualization inserts itself into the flow of communications from devices such as the following:

- Terminals
- Desktop PCs
- Laptop PCs
- Netbooks
- Tablets
- Thin clients
- Smartphones
- Other network-enabled intelligent devices, such as a point-of-sale device or laboratory instrument

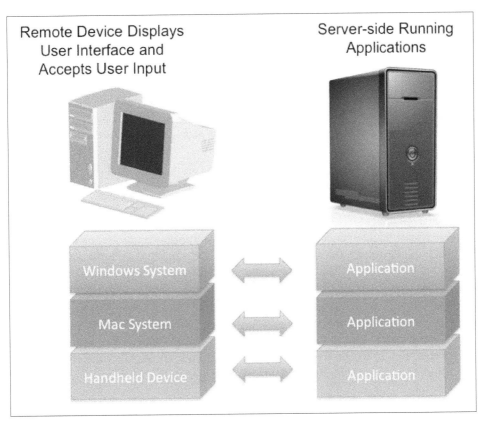

Figure 2-2. Access virtualization at work

Access virtualization technology makes it possible for the remote device to display the user interface of a remote application and accept keyboard, mouse, and other input from the user.

The flow continues to applications or workloads running on the following types of devices:

- Physical systems
- Virtual systems (virtual desktop, virtual client, or virtual server)

This intervention allows individuals to access applications running anywhere, on any type of system, over nearly any type of network—without devices on either side of the conversation knowing too much about what's happening on the other side. This type of technology is often used to allow devices to access applications running in virtual processing environments (see Chapter 4 for more information).

When Is Access Virtualization the Right Choice?

When organizations are attempting to achieve the following goals, access virtualization technology is the best choice:

Greater agility
> When organizations need mobile staff members to have the ability to access applications and data from wherever they are and would rather not provide them with a general-purpose system having its own storage, applications, and the like.

Device independence
> When staff members need the ability to access applications and data using many different types of devices, without the organization being forced to rewrite applications or change how or where data is stored.

Improved availability
> When staff members need the ability to access applications and data even if their access-point devices fail or are out of service for some reason. Staff members can simply access needed applications from another device using access virtualization.

Greater security
> When organizations are trying to prevent worms, viruses, and other forms of malware from entering the data center, access virtualization provides an additional level of security. The remote device may not have the ability to store data—making transmission of worms and viruses difficult or impossible. All of the actual application execution (application, database, storage, and other processing) happens remotely.

Cost reduction
> When organizations are doing their best to reduce the costs of provisioning client systems, installing client software, updating client software, and the like, access virtualization makes it possible to do all of this from a central location. It is also possible to fix problems from a central location.

Access to cloud computing software as a service (SaaS) applications
> Some SaaS offerings download a sophisticated client that runs inside of the web browser that runs inside of the remote device. This approach can also be thought of as access virtualization. (Cloud computing, such as software as a service, is not the focus of this book, however.)

Players in the Access Virtualization World

Although there are many players in the access virtualization market, a short summary of the most important suppliers follows:

Citrix (http://citrix.com/)
> Citrix offers virtualization technology in a number of different categories. One of the company's earliest products was called Mainframe. It allowed a number of

different types of client systems to access Windows and Solaris (UNIX) applications. Over time, the product was renamed MetaFrame, and it is now known as XenApp.

Microsoft (http://www.microsoft.com/)
Microsoft started including access virtualization capabilities in its operating systems as far back as Windows 95 and Windows NT Server. The company's technology was not sold separately. The capability was called Microsoft Terminal Services.

HP, IBM, Sun (now Oracle), and all other suppliers of UNIX
X-Windows has been a standard part of the UNIX operating system since shortly after the Athena Project was completed at MIT. X-Windows Servers, as the client portions of the X-Windows system are called, are available for nearly all client systems.

Red Hat, SUSE, and all other Linux distributions
Linux has provided capabilities compatible with X-Windows since the first commercial distributions of the software were made available. X-Windows Servers that support UNIX typically will support Linux environments as well.

A Few Examples of Access Virtualization in Use

There are many different environments in which access virtualization can be beneficial. The following list contains only a few examples.

Health care
Health care regulations, such as the Health Insurance Portability and Accountability Act of 1996 (HIPAA) in the United States, require that health care providers ensure that personal data is not disclosed accidentally. When doctors, nurses, therapists, and other health care workers access patient data, the organization must make sure that patient data is protected. This also means that this data cannot be left on access point devices, such as smartphones, PCs, laptops, or tablets. One way to be certain that these regulations are followed is to make sure that patient data never permanently resides on these devices. Access virtualization products simplify compliance by allowing organizations to keep the applications and their data back in the data center.

Task-oriented workers
Task-oriented workers often use computers as part of their work. For the most part, they are not interested in how the computers operate. Rather than giving these staff members PCs or laptops, some organizations provide a much simpler device: a thin client, or a PC or laptop set up to run only the access virtualization client. Staff members can easily access the applications and data needed for the task at hand without becoming computer administrators or operators. This approach drastically lowers the administrative costs of system management, software

installation, and software updating and it allows support to be provided from a central location.

Non-computer-focused knowledge workers

Many knowledge workers, such as doctors, attorneys, and managers, use computers as part of their work. They often are not interested in understanding, in any detail, how their systems work. As with the task-oriented workers, organizations often find it easier to provide these staff members with access to centralized computing without putting general-purpose systems on their desks.

CHAPTER 3

Application Virtualization: Application Isolation, Delivery and Performance

What Is Application Virtualization?

Let's dive one level lower into the model (see Figure 3-1). Application virtualization has two forms: client-side application virtualization and server-side application virtualization. Application virtualization runs on top of the operating systems that manage the functioning of systems. It makes it possible for an application to be "encapsulated" or run in an artificial environment.

The major difference between access virtualization and application virtualization is that a portion, or perhaps all, of the application actually runs on the local device rather than on a remote server. The encapsulated application still requires support functions offered by a specific operating system, so this means, for example, that encapsulated Windows applications need to be executed on a remote Windows device. This is different, by the way, from processing virtualization (see Chapter 4 for more information on processing virtualization), which isolates a workload from either the operating system or physical system it is running on.

As with other virtualization technologies, application virtualization has a long track record of success. The earliest forms of application virtualization were developed by mainframe suppliers, such as IBM, Burroughs (now part of Unisys), and others, as a structured form of application development and deployment. At that time, "transaction processing monitor" was the industry catchphrase for server-side application virtualization tools.

Windows has been the center of intense development of application virtualization as well. AppZero, Citrix, Microsoft, VMware, and others have been offering client-side and/or server-side application virtualization since the early 1990s.

Today, this type of virtualization is often used in conjunction with various forms of processing virtualization, which will be examined in Chapter 4.

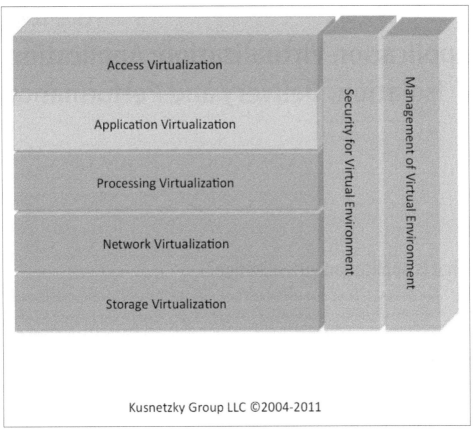

Figure 3-1. *Application virtualization*

What Does Application Virtualization Do?

As shown in Figure 3-2, there are two different forms of application virtualization, client-side and server-side. They make it possible for applications to run in a protected, isolated, or artificial environment.

Let's examine each type in turn:

Client-side application virtualization

    The client-side form of application virtualization creates a protected environment that makes it possible for applications to be isolated from one another and from the base operating system. This means that applications that could not successfully reside on the same client system could be used together. This prevents the "library version mismatch" problem with Windows applications.

    It also means that an application designed for an earlier version of the operating system may continue to function on a newer version of that operating system, even though it would be incompatible without being placed in a virtual environment.

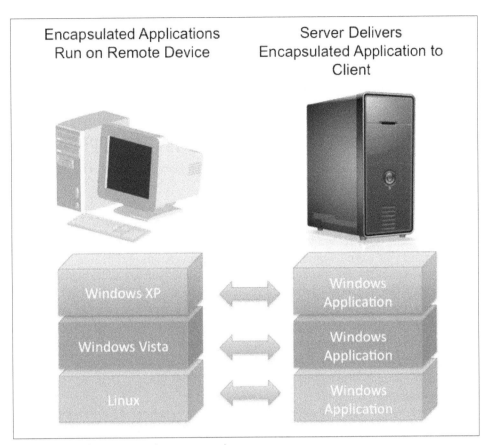

Figure 3-2. Application virtualization at work

This is very useful when an organization is in the process of upgrading from one operating system version to another and can't upgrade the application.

Another use is delivering applications or application components to a target client system as needed. Application virtualization also makes it possible for those applications or application components to either remain on the client system for later use or be automatically removed after they have been used.

Server-side application virtualization

Placing server-side applications in a virtual environment offers many of the same benefits as client-side application virtualization. Applications that are normally incompatible with one another can be made to work together. Applications that might be incompatible with new versions of an operating system can continue to be used.

Server-side application virtualization offers a few other valuable functions as well. Multiple instances of an application can be automatically started on other machines when the workload is no longer meeting service-level guidelines. This could mean faster performance or being able to handle workload requests from a larger number of people.

Another important benefit is that applications can be restarted upon failure. While this is not the same thing as a high availability cluster (a processing virtualization function that will be described in Chapter 4), it can be very valuable.

When Is Application Virtualization a Suggested Approach?

Application virtualization is the best choice if the organization has one of the following goals:

Greater application isolation
Organizations need to make incompatible applications run side-by-side on the same system. This requirement can arise when the applications were purchased from third parties and require support of different versions of the same tools. Typically new versions of application development and runtime tools replace older versions when they are installed. This can cause older applications to fail.

Operating system independence
Applications designed for an earlier version of an operation must be made to work with a newer version. Running applications in a virtual environment can significantly extend the life cycle of an application, giving the organization time to update the application or find a replacement for the application.

Improved availability
Applications provide critical functions and the organization will suffer great harm if those functions become unavailable for any reason. Applications can be made to fail over from one server to another.

Improved performance or scalability
Applications must perform faster or be able to service larger numbers of users. Server-based application virtualization products often include a workload management function, allowing the same application to automatically be started on multiple systems, to either improve application performance or allow more people to access the application simultaneously.

Cost reduction
It is necessary to reduce the cost for provisioning, installation, updating, and administrating applications. It is far easier and less costly to provision systems, install software, update software, and the like if it can be done from a central location. Once encapsulated, or placed in a virtual environment, applications can more easily be copied to remote systems or streamed to remote systems when required.

Players in the Application Virtualization World

Although there are many players in the application virtualization market, a short summary of the most important suppliers follows:

Citrix (http://www.citrix.com)
> Citrix offers virtualization technology in a number of different categories. The company's XenApp is considered an application virtualization, too. XenApp is a client-side application virtualization product.

Microsoft (http://www.microsoft.com)
> Microsoft acquired Softricity in July 2006 and enhanced its product, renaming it SoftGrid. It is now called Microsoft Application Virtualization or App-V. App-V provides both client- and server-side application virtualization functions.

VMware (http://www.vmware.com)
> VMware acquired ThinApp from Thinstall in January 2008. ThinApp is a client-side application virtualization function.

AppZero (http://www.appzero.com)
> AppZero makes it possible for organizations to encapsulate applications into a virtual application environment (VAA). VAAs can be easily delivered to one or more servers.

A Few Examples of Application Virtualization in Use

There are many different environments in which application virtualization can be beneficial. The following list contains only a few examples:

Operating system updates
> When new versions of operating systems are released, they often include enhancements that prevent older software from operating properly. A properly encapsulated application, one that has been placed in a virtual environment, may continue to function as expected. The operating system sees a "current application" and the application sees the proper operating system.

Application delivery and protection
> An organization may wish to deliver applications and application updates to its staff, consultants, or customers in an encapsulated or virtual form. The application may either be copied to the client system or be streamed down as needed. Applications can then be set to run only at specific times, from specific locations, and even to disable themselves after a certain date.

CHAPTER 4

Processing Virtualization: Doing System Tricks

What Is Processing Virtualization?

Ready to dive one more level deeper into the model? Processing virtualization (see Figure 4-1) has five forms: parallel processing monitors, workload management monitors, high availability/fail over/disaster recovery monitors, virtual machine software, and operating system virtualization and partitioning. Parallel processing, workload management, and high availability configurations are commonly called "clusters," even though they serve different purposes. Although some forms of processing virtualization, such as virtual machine software and operating system virtualization and partitioning software, seem similar (see Chapter 3 for more information on application virtualization), processing virtualization operates at or below the operating system.

Processing virtualization does one of three things: encapsulates the operating system so that many virtual systems can run on a single system, links multiple systems together so that workloads will fail over if a system fails, or links systems together so an application or data can be spread across all of them for performance or scalability. This means that, depending upon the type of processing virtualization, the application can be run on multiple systems simultaneously or run under a hypervisor. A hypervisor can run as a process under another operating system or can run directly on the system hardware. Hypervisors can support one or more complete virtual systems at the same time.

This technology, as with other virtualization technologies, was originally developed for mainframe systems in the late 1960s, was recreated on minicomputers (now called midrange machines) in the 1980s, and started appearing on industry-standard systems (X86-based) in the early 1990s.

This type of virtualization is often used in conjunction with several other types.

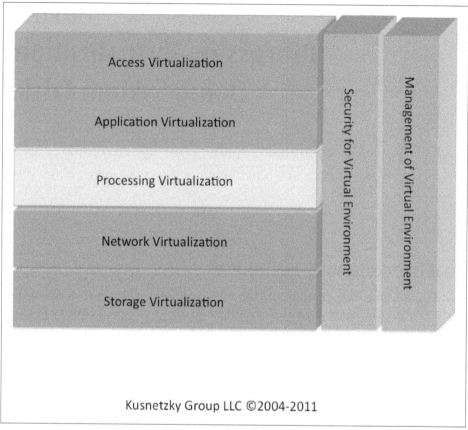

Figure 4-1. Processing virtualization

What Does Processing Virtualization Do?

As shown in Figure 4-2, there are many different forms of processing virtualization. They make it possible for either a single system to appear to be many or many systems appear to be a single system.

Let's examine each type in turn:

Making one system appear to be many (see Figure 4-3)

Virtual machine software allows the entire stack of software that makes up a system to be encapsulated into a virtual machine file. Then a hypervisor can run one or more complete virtual systems on a physical machine. There are two types of hypervisors: A type 1 hypervisor runs on top of the physical system. A type 2 hypervisor allows a guest system to run as a process under another operating system. Each of these systems processes as if it has total control of its own system, even though it may only be using a portion of the capabilities of a larger physical system.

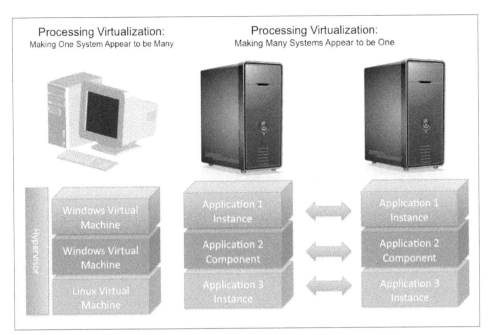

Figure 4-2. Processing virtualization at work

Operating system virtualization and partitioning allows many applications to run under a single operating system and gives each a completely isolated, protected environment. Each application functions as if it is running on its own system and is managing its own resources.

Making many systems appear to be one

Parallel processing monitors make it possible for many machines to execute the same applications or application components, with the goal of reducing the processing time of the application. Each system is asked to process one segment of data or run a single application component. As it finishes its task, the parallel processing monitor passes it another task to complete. This computational approach allows applications to complete hundreds, thousands, or, perhaps, tens of thousands times faster.

Workload management monitors (also known as *load balancing monitors*) make it possible for multiple instances of a single application to run simultaneously on many machines. As requests are made, the workload monitor sends each to the system having the most available capacity. While each application may run no more quickly than before, more people can be served by the application.

High availability/fail over/disaster recovery monitors make it possible for people using a computing service to be protected from an application, system, or system component failure. The monitor detects a failure and restarts an application to a surviving system.

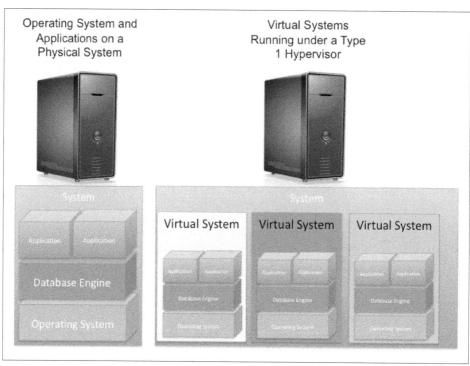

Figure 4-3. Physical versus virtual servers

Memory virtualization or *distributed cache memory* makes it possible for many systems to share their internal memory. This capability is at the heart of the many non-relational databases known collectively as *NoSQL databases.*

When Is Processing Virtualization the Preferred Approach?

Processing virtualization is the best choice if the organization is pursuing the following goals:

Greater application isolation
> The organization needs to have different workloads or applications share the same machine, even though those workloads or applications were developed to run under different versions of the same operating system, say Windows Server 2003 and Windows Server 2008. Virtual machine software, a form of processing virtualization, makes it possible to run several different operating systems on the same physical system simultaneously.

Operating system independence
> The organization needs to have different workloads or applications share the same machine, even though those workloads or applications were developed to run

under different operating systems, say Windows Server 2008 and Linux. Virtual machine software, a form of processing virtualization, makes it possible to run several different operating systems on the same physical system simultaneously.

Improved availability

Applications must remain available even though components or complete systems have failed. This can be achieved using three different processing virtualization technologies: high availability/fail over/disaster recovery monitors, workload management monitors, or virtual machine software combined with a special form of management software. Complete system environments can be made to fail over from one physical system to another.

Improved performance or scalability

The organization needs a single application to run faster than is possible using a single system. In this case, parallel processing software can be used to harness the computational power of many physical or virtual systems to handle tasks significantly faster or significantly larger than a single system could manage.

Cost reduction

The organization needs to reduce the overall cost of hardware, reduce power consumption, and/or reduce system administrative costs. Virtual machine or operating system virtualization and partitioning software could be used to move multiple physical system workloads onto a single physical machine. While this can reduce the overall costs of hardware, power, or system administration, it may not reduce the overall costs of administrations, operations, or software.

Optimization

The organization needs to manage costs by optimizing the use of physical systems. Virtual machine or operating system virtualization and partitioning software can be used to bring many workloads together on a single machine. The goal is to bring workloads having different peak usage patterns together on a single physical machine. If done correctly, idle time for one workload is the busy time for another.

Players in the Processing Virtualization World

Although there are many players in the processing virtualization market, a short summary of the most important suppliers follows:

Citrix (http://www.citrix.com)

Citrix offers virtualization technology in a number of different categories. Citrix acquired XenSource. The company's XenServer is a hypervisor. The company also offers workload management software.

Microsoft (http://www.microsoft.com)

Microsoft acquired Connectix in February 2003. The company's product was renamed Hyper-V and has been enhanced significantly over the years. Microsoft also offers parallel processing, workload management, and high availability/fail over/ disaster recovery software.

VMware (http://www.vmware.com)
VMware offers a hypervisor called ESX Server. It has developed virtual machine migration software and automation software that functions as a high availability/ fail over/disaster recovery product.

A Few Examples of Processing Virtualization in Use

There are many different environments in which processing virtualization can be beneficial. The following list contains only a few examples.

Parallel processing monitor
Modeling of financial transactions, architectural models, and creation of digital content is very processing intensive. Parallel processing monitors are used to harness the power of many physical systems to create a single, very-high-performance computing environment.

Workload management monitor
Organizations needing to support enormous transactional workloads, such as an ecommerce site, use workload managers to allow their order entry application to run on many physical systems. This makes it possible for hundreds of thousands or, perhaps, millions of customers to be serviced simultaneously.

High availability/fail over/disaster recovery monitor
Applications that cannot be allowed to fail or slow down may be hosted on several systems simultaneously. If a system, the application, or some application component doesn't meet service-level objectives, the application can be automatically restarted on another system. Another use of this technology is to allow multiple systems to shadow the functions of a primary system. If that primary system fails, the backup systems can complete the transactions in flight. The end users are unaware of a failure.

Virtual machine software
Organizations wish to make optimal use of their physical systems, but they need to make applications supported by many different operating system versions or operating systems function side by side. This is the approach commonly selected for industry-standard system workloads, even though operating system virtualization and partitioning might be a better choice in many situations.

Operating system virtualization and partitioning software
When all of an organization's applications are designed to work with a single operating system, it might be more efficient to use operating system virtualization and partitioning rather than virtual machine software to provide the application isolation and system optimization needed. This is the approach usually selected for mainframe and midrange system workloads.

CHAPTER 5

Network Virtualization: Controlling the View of the Network

What Is Network Virtualization?

Our journey into the layers of virtualization continues. This time, we're going to examine the concept of network virtualization (see Figure 5-1). Network virtualization refers to tools used to present an artificial view of the network environment.

Network virtualization often is supported by network routers, network servers, and the like. Systems executing the organization's applications and workloads may not know this is happening. Client systems and server systems just see the network as presented by those network resources.

This technology, as with other virtualization technologies, was originally developed for mainframe systems in the late 1960s, was recreated on minicomputers (now called midrange machines) in the 1980s, and started appearing on industry-standard systems (X86-based) in the early 1990s. One difference is that network virtualization often was implemented on separate network servers rather than inside the operating systems supporting clients or servers.

This type of virtualization is often used in conjunction with several other types.

What Does Network Virtualization Do?

As shown in Figure 5-2, network virtualization creates an artificial view of the network that hides the physical network from clients and servers. It provides the following functions:

Network routing
> Network traffic directed to remote clients or servers is sent from network to network until it reaches the target systems.

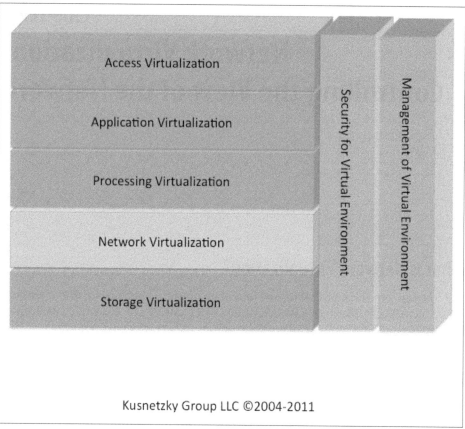

Figure 5-1. Network virtualization

Network address translation

One network address may actually be used by a number of network clients or servers. A network address translation layer sends network messages from and to the right client or server systems. This means that a network service provider could provide a single Internet protocol address (IP address) for an entire facility and all of the clients and servers in that facility would still be able to send and receive messages to outside resources.

Network isolation

Clients and servers may only be allowed to see (and thus communicate with) specific systems. This reduces the possibility of the data center becoming infected with worms, viruses, or other malware.

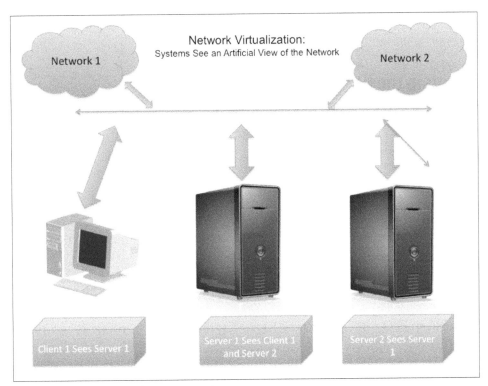

Figure 5-2. Network virtualization at work

When Is Network Virtualization Required?

When organizations have the following goals, network virtualization technology is the best solution:

Improving network reliability
> When the organization needs constant network access in a data center, two or more physical networks supplied by different providers are typically installed. Network virtualization makes it possible for network communications to fail over from one network to the other in the case of a failure.

Improving network performance
> Increased network throughput can be achieved if several, or perhaps all, outside network communications links are used simultaneously to improve overall network performance as well as to increase network scalability.

Improving network security
> If network security is a key requirement, the data center network can be configured as several secure zones. Only specific network traffic may cross from one zone to another or from the internal network to the external network. This reduces the

possibility of clients or servers being infected by worms, viruses, or other malware. It is also possible to allow clients to only see servers they are allowed to access, even though other network resources are available.

Players in the Network Virtualization World

Although there are many players in the network virtualization market, a short summary of some of these suppliers follows:

Cisco (http://www.cisco.com)
Cisco offers a number of network servers that perform network virtualization functions.

HP (http://www.hp.com)
HP offers network virtualization functions as part of its general-purpose server operating systems and also offers network servers providing those functions.

IBM (http://www.ibm.com)
IBM offers network virtualization functions as part of its general-purpose server operating systems and also offers network servers providing those functions.

Juniper Systems (http://www.junipersys.com)
Juniper offers a number of network servers that perform network virtualization functions.

A Few Examples of Network Virtualization in Use

There are many different environments in which network virtualization can be beneficial. The following list contains only a few examples:

Increasing performance or scale of network-centric workloads
A transaction-oriented ecommerce application might overwhelm the capacity of a single network link, so an organization may install many network links from the same or different suppliers. Network virtualization would make optimal use of these resources.

Data center security
Network virtualization can be used to isolate the internal network from all of the external networks in use. Only authorized network traffic is allowed to enter and leave the data center network.

High availability/fail over/disaster recovery
Organizations may install network links from many different suppliers. If any link fails, the network virtualization function would reroute messages from the failed network connection to one of the surviving network connections.

Physical and network resources devoted to department or business unit

Some regulated industries require that sensitive or personal information be maintained on separate systems and networks. Network virtualization makes it possible to segment a single network into multiple independent networks without requiring the organization to install separate wiring and networking equipment.

CHAPTER 6

Storage Virtualization: Where Are Your Files and Applications?

What Is Storage Virtualization?

Our journey into the layers of virtualization continues and we have reached the bottom of the model. The remaining two layers of virtualization technology touch all of the others. This time, we're going to examine storage virtualization (see Figure 6-1). Storage virtualization refers to the tools used to present an artificial view of the storage environment.

Storage virtualization often is supported by storage servers. Clients and servers need not know where the files they're processing really reside. They also need not know what type of storage device holds their applications and data. The storage devices could be based on rotating media, such as traditional disk drives, or solid state technology, such as SSDs or dynamic random access memory (DRAM).

Once again, this technology was originally developed for mainframe systems in the late 1960s, was recreated on minicomputers (now called midrange machines) in the 1980s, and started appearing on industry-standard systems (X86-based) in the early 1980s. The industry is still in the middle of a transition from server- or client-attached storage to virtual storage that is located in the network.

This type of virtualization is often used in conjunction with several other types.

What Does Storage Virtualization Do?

As shown in Figure 6-2, storage virtualization creates an artificial view of the network that hides the physical network from clients and servers. It provides the following functions:

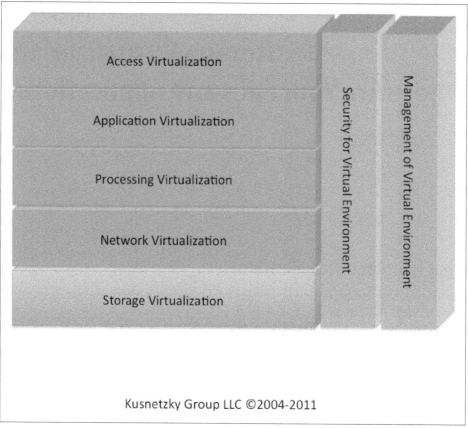

Inside the figure:
Access Virtualization

Application Virtualization

Processing Virtualization

Network Virtualization

Storage Virtualization

Security for Virtual Environment

Management of Virtual Environment

Kusnetzky Group LLC ©2004-2011

Figure 6-1. Storage virtualization

Allowing distributed file systems
> Remote storage devices are made to look like they were directly attached to the system. The local system does not know where they are located or what type of storage device they are.

Creating artificial storage volumes
> Multiple storage devices can be harnessed together to create the image of a single, much larger storage device.

Creating arrays of storage volumes
> Applications and data can be spread over a number of storage devices and storage servers to improve overall storage performance. This function can also be used to improve storage reliability. The same data can be stored on several storage devices or storage servers. If one storage device or server fails, the data can be reconstructed.

Allowing greater control of storage space
> Storage devices can be segmented into several "file systems," allowing the storage device to be more fully utilized.

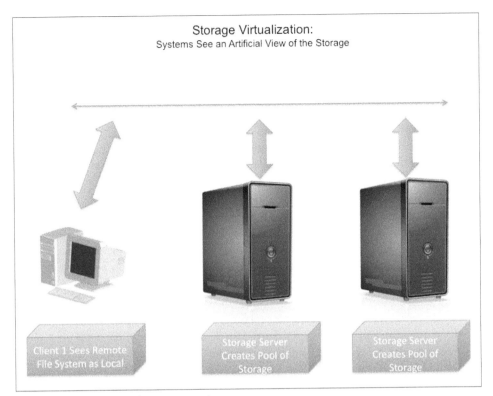

Figure 6-2. *Storage virtualization at work*

Allowing incompatible systems to share storage devices

Mainframes, single-vendor operating systems, Windows, Linux, and UNIX all use different mechanisms to store and retrieve applications and data. Storage virtualization makes it possible for all of these to share the same storage devices and the files they contain.

Storage servers are, by the way, computer systems managing a number of storage devices. This allows many general-purpose systems to access the same storage. The storage server's operating system keeps track of which general-purpose server is allowed to access what data storage on individual storage devices. If these storage servers connect to the general-purpose systems over a special-purpose storage network, the configuration is often called a *storage area network* (SAN). Storage accessed over a network is called *network attached storage* (NAS), regardless of whether it is on a SAN or the same local area network (LAN) used by general-purpose systems.

When Should Storage Virtualization Be Used?

Storage virtualization should be used by organizations seeking to achieve the following goals:

High availability/fail over/disaster recovery
> If organizations are deploying application or processing virtualization, it is likely that storage virtualization should also be deployed. When organizations need continuous access to applications and data, if a single storage device, the network used to access that device, or the storage server fails, storage virtualization can press another device, network, or storage server into service.

Improve storage performance
> If application virtualization, workload management, or parallel processing software is deployed to increase overall scalability or performance, storage virtualization should be deployed, too. Today's distributed applications often assign the same task to many systems. Many systems working together on a single task can overwhelm the storage system. If the workload is spread over many different storage devices, the workload can be handled.

Making the same storage resource serve everyone
> If the organization is deploying many virtual environments, each running on a different type of operating system, storage virtualization should be deployed as well. Organizations typically have a large number of different applications. Each of them may be hosted on a different physical or virtual system. Each of the applications may be hosted on a different operating system, each of which uses storage differently. Storage virtualization is used to make the same storage devices serve many tasks.

Players in the Storage Virtualization World

Although there are many players in the storage virtualization market, a short summary of some of the suppliers follows:

EMC (http://www.emc.com)
> EMC began as a company offering third-party memory boards and storage devices for mainframes and minicomputers. Over time, the company created storage servers that could serve the storage needs of many different types of systems.

Hitachi (http://www.hds.com)
> Hitachi offers storage devices and storage servers for mainframes, midrange systems, and industry-standard systems.

HP (http://www.hp.com)
> HP offers its own storage servers to support its midrange systems and industry-standard systems.

IBM (http://www.ibm.com)

IBM has offered its own mainframes, midrange systems, and industry-standard servers. The company offers storage servers and storage devices that can serve the needs of all of its products.

NetApp (http://www.netapp.com)

NetApp has long offered storage servers for industry-standard systems and mid-range systems from many suppliers.

A Few Examples of Storage Virtualization in Use

There are many different environments in which storage virtualization can be beneficial. The following list contains only a few examples:

Increasing performance or scale of storage-centric workloads

A transaction-oriented ecommerce application might overwhelm the capacity of a single storage system, so an organization typically spreads the applications and data over a number of storage devices and storage servers. Another approach is to substitute special, high-speed storage technology with devices that use solid state devices (SSD) or dynamic random access memory (DRAM) rather than a spinning disk. These devices may provide latency and throughput similar to the system's own internal memory.

Data center optimization

If each server had its own private storage system, a great deal of space would be taken up in the organization's data center for storage devices. Furthermore, it is likely that these storage devices would be lightly used; that is, a great deal of empty space would be found on each device. To reduce overall costs for storage devices, data center space, power, and heat production, organizations use storage virtualization to share storage devices among all of the servers supporting a given workload.

High availability/fail over/disaster recovery

Organizations may install redundant storage servers. If any storage device or storage server fails, the storage virtualization function would reroute requests from the failed devices to one of the surviving storage devices or servers.

CHAPTER 7

Security for Virtual Environments: Guarding the Treasure

What Is Security for Virtual Environments?

There are two segments of the Kusnetzky Group Model that cut across all of the functional segments. Security and management for virtual environments protect and manage all of the other layers. This time, we're going to examine security for virtual environments (see Figure 7-1). Security for virtual environments refers to the tools necessary to control access to and use of all of the other layers of virtualization technology.

Depending upon the approach, security can require a small piece of software, often called an *agent*, to be added to each virtual resource. This, of course, can be quite a task in itself. This approach also means that part of each system's time is spent doing security processing. If we consider a physical system supporting 40 virtual servers, each of which is supporting multiple workloads and communicating to thousands of client systems, the task of installing and maintaining all of that security software could be an overwhelming task.

Other suppliers have developed a different approach. Their approach is to capture the stream of network communication going from server to server, from application to application, from storage device to server, and funnel it through a separate security appliance server. This way, a great deal of processing can be done on each stream of communication to filter out worms, viruses, malware, and the like. This function is often combined with other management functions, such as configuration management, performance management, or automation of tasks. This approach does not require that agents be installed on each resource.

This technology is a far more recent addition to virtualized environments. It started to appear in the late 1980s as a way to protect midrange and industry-standard systems from intrusions coming from the network.

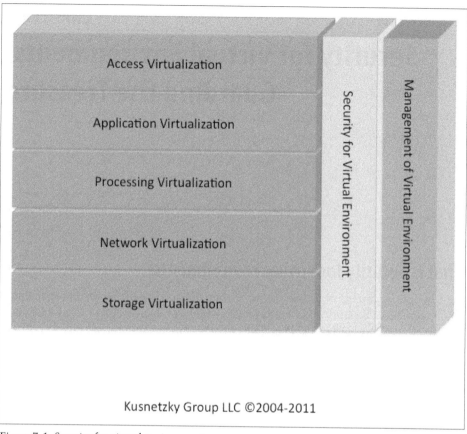

Figure 7-1. *Security for virtual environments*

What Does Security for Virtual Environments Do?

Security for virtual environments guards access to each of the layers of virtualization found in an organization.

It is best if security for virtualized environments is part of the architecture (that is, part of the plan, rather than added on later). As systems become increasingly complex, they expose more interfaces, sometimes called "surface area," to the network and, thus, to potential attackers.

When Is Security for Virtual Environments Needed?

The goals of security in a virtual environment are really simple. This layer is meant to protect all information and computing resources so that only authorized use is made of them. While simple in concept, this is exceedingly difficult to accomplish in reality.

As each new application or layer of virtualization technology is added, there are new areas to attack. Organizations should consider security when moving functions into a virtual environment and then deploy the appropriate security tools.

Players in the Security for Virtual Environments World

Although there are many players in the security for virtual environments market, a short summary of some of the suppliers follows:

CA (http://www.ca.com)
> CA has long been a major player in security. It is natural as virtual environments become more popular that CA would enhance its products to protect them.

Cisco (http://www.cisco.com)
> Cisco offers security products that work in conjunction with its network virtualization servers and, more recently, with its unified computing systems (UCS).

HP (http://www.hp.com)
> HP has offered security products for its computing environments for a long time.

IBM Tivoli (http://www.ibm.com/software/tivoli/)
> Tivoli, like CA, has been a security player for many years.

Juniper Systems (http://www.junipersys.com)
> Juniper, like Cisco, offers security products that work in conjunction with its network virtualization servers.

A Few Examples of Security for Virtual Environments in Use

There are many different environments in which security for virtual environments can be beneficial. The following list contains only a few examples:

Access virtualization
> When remote devices are accessing applications through access virtualization, security technology on the server can monitor attempts to connect to the server and overall application usage. This technology ensures that access is allowed only to authorized individuals, using appropriate devices, at authorized times, and only from authorized places. Usually this function is based on a directory of computing resources, individuals, and roles within the company.

Application virtualization
> The encapsulation technology used in application virtualization may contain tools that communicate with directory and security services back at the remote server. The encapsulated application can disable itself if it finds that it has been asked to run on the wrong system, at the wrong time, or from some unknown part of the network. The application virtualization technology would disable the encapsulated

application and report the attempted misuse to the remote systems security monitoring system so that it can be logged.

Processing virtualization

In processing virtualization configurations, security monitoring can determine if anyone attempts unauthorized use of computing resources, regardless of whether they are physical or virtual. Only authorized individuals would be able to use applications managed by workload managers/load balancers, virtual desktops, virtual servers, or clustered servers.

Storage virtualization

Security software can monitor access to storage devices and storage servers. Only authorized applications or servers would be allowed access to information resources.

Network virtualization

Security monitors can monitor network traffic and only allow authorized users, applications, or systems to send and receive messages. Unauthorized users or systems would not be able to use the network, even if physically attached to the network.

CHAPTER 8

Management for Virtual Environments

What Is Management for Virtual Environments?

Two segments of the model cut across all of the functional segments. Security and management for virtual environments protect and manage all of the other layers. This time, we're going to examine management for virtual environments (see Figure 8-1). Management for virtual environments refers to the tools necessary to install virtual environments and to watch, analyze, control, automate, and optimize what they are doing.

As virtual environments become more and more complex, this layer of virtualization technology becomes more and more important. We have already reached a point at which human operators cannot track what is happening in real time and respond before there is a slowdown or failure.

Technology used for management of virtual environments includes the following functions:

- Creating virtual environments or components of virtual environments
- Provisioning those environments or components
- Monitoring their execution
- Controlling execution of virtual environments or components
- Analyzing execution log data to find configuration, performance, or operational issues
- Optimizing use of virtual environments or components
- Automating use of virtual environments or components

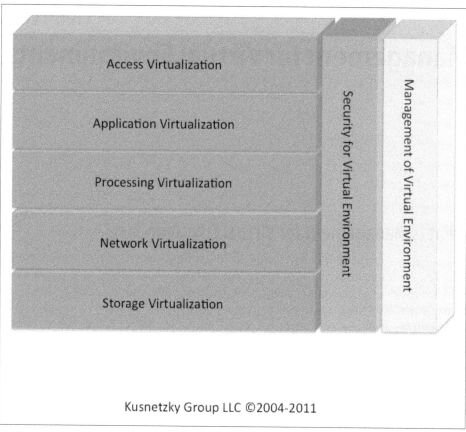

Figure 8-1. Management for virtual environments

What Does Management for Virtual Environments Do?

Management for virtual environments guards access to each of the layers of virtualization found in an organization.

Virtualized client resources

- Creation of client-side virtual machine images and setting the proper parameters (virtual memory, number of virtual processors, virtual storage size, etc.)
- Installation of operating systems, setting up the proper parameters, and installing updates
- Setting user personalization (desktop images, preferred desktop icons, etc.)

- Configuring user data
- Installation of applications, moving necessary data, and adjusting application configuration settings

Virtualized server resources

- Creation of server-side virtual machine images and setting proper parameters (virtual memory, number of virtual processors, virtual storage size, etc.)
- Installation of operating systems, setting up proper parameters, and installing updates
- Installation of applications, moving necessary data, and adjusting application configuration settings
- Workload management; that is, sending user requests to one of a number of systems depending upon which system has the most available capacity
- Automation of virtual environment workloads; that is, staging applications so that they don't start until the necessary data is available or dealing with an application failure
- Managing policies that guide the functioning of the virtual environment; that is, telling the system the requirements of each job, when jobs can run, who is allowed to use them, where they are allowed to run, and performance requirements
- Orchestration of server workloads; that is, moving tasks from system to system as required to meet service-level objectives or handle failures

It is best if management for virtualized environments is part of the architecture (that is, part of the plan, rather than added on later). As systems become increasingly complex, they require more and more attention to real-time events.

When Is Management Software for Virtual Environments Needed?

Whenever an organization embarks on the journey to a virtual environment, it is important to also deploy the technology that manages creation of virtual resources, provisions those resources, monitors the environment's operation, automates functions to reduce the need for manual intervention, and creates an optimal environment that complies with the organization's service-level goals and other policies.

Players in the Management for Virtual Environments World

A new player in management for virtual environments comes to my attention almost every day. Although there are many players, a short summary of some of the suppliers follows:

CA (http://www.ca.com)
> CA has long been a major player in management software. It is natural that, as virtual environments became more popular, CA would enhance its products to manage those environments.

HP (http://www.hp.com)
> HP has offered management products for its computing environments for a long time.

IBM Tivoli (http://www.ibm.com/software/tivoli/)
> Tivoli has been a management player for many years. It, too, has brought its products into virtual environments.

A Few Examples of Management for Virtual Environments in Use

There are many different environments in which management for virtual environments can be beneficial. The following list contains only a few examples:

Access virtualization
> Management technology provisions clients, monitors usage, and ensures that access is performing properly. Failures and slowdowns are prevented when possible and failover routines are executed when failure occurs.

Application virtualization
> Access to applications and application components is provisioned, monitored, and controlled so that they are configured properly, they run optimally, and slowdowns and failures are prevented. As with access virtualization, failover routines are executed when a failure occurs.

Processing virtualization
> Access to computing resources, regardless of whether they are physical or virtual, is provisioned, monitored, and controlled so that resources are configured properly, they run optimally, and slowdowns and failures are prevented. As with access virtualization, failover routines are executed when a failure occurs.

Storage virtualization
> Storage resources are provisioned, monitored, and controlled so that they are configured properly, they run optimally, and slowdowns and failures are prevented. As with other layers of virtualization, failover routines are executed when a failure occurs.

Network virtualization

Network resources are provisioned, monitored, and controlled so that they are configured properly, they run optimally, and slowdowns and failures are prevented. As with other layers of virtualization, failover routines are executed when a failure occurs.

Security for virtual environments

Security services are provisioned, monitored, and controlled so that they are configured properly, they run optimally, and slowdowns and failures are prevented. As with other layers of virtualization, failover routines are executed when a failure occurs.

CHAPTER 9

Using Virtualization: The Right Tool for the Job

Highlighting When Use Cases Are Confused with Technology

Media reports often confuse base virtualization technology with specific use cases or instances of use of virtualization technology. So, for example, when virtual machine technology, one of the five types of processing virtualization, is used, media reports might discuss that as either server virtualization or desktop virtualization. The use of application virtualization, processing virtualization, or storage virtualization might be discussed as "clustering." Let's examine a few use cases or instances and see what technology is really being used:

- "Big data"
- Clusters
- Desktop virtualization
- High-performance computing
- Server virtualization
- Extreme transaction processing

This chapter is meant to examine industry catchphrases and quickly review which parts of the virtualization model are actually in use. Please refer to the chapter on each of those topics for more information.

Big Data

"Big data" (see Figure 9-1), a specific use of a combination of processing virtualization and storage virtualization, is a catchphrase that has been bubbling up from the high-performance computing niche of the IT market (more about that later in this chapter). Yes, this configuration is a cluster (see the next section) that is being used specifically to manage extremely large stores of rapidly changing data.

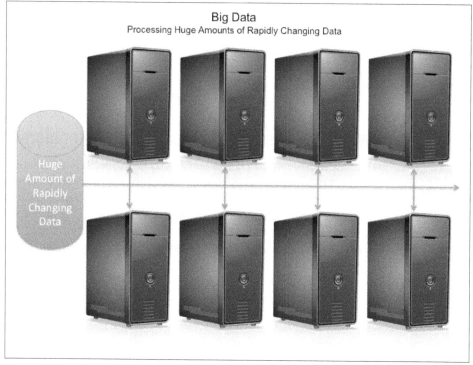

Figure 9-1. Big data

Increasingly suppliers of processing virtualization and storage virtualization software have begun to flog "big data" in their presentations. What, exactly, does this phrase mean? If you sit through the presentations of ten suppliers of technology, fifteen different definitions are likely to come forward. Each definition, of course, tends to support the need for that supplier's products and services. (Imagine that.) In simplest terms, the phrase refers to tools, processes, and procedures that allow an organization to create, manipulate, and manage very large data sets and storage facilities.

Does this mean terabytes, petabytes, or even larger collections of data? The answer offered by these suppliers is "yes." They would go on to say that you need their products to manage and make best use of that mass of data. Managing huge, dynamic sets of data can be problematic without the appropriate tools and processes.

An example often cited is the mass of weather data collected daily by the U.S. National Oceanic and Atmospheric Administration (NOAA) to aid in climate, ecosystem, weather, and commercial research. Add that to the masses of data collected by the U.S. National Aeronautics and Space Administration (NASA) for its research, and the numbers get pretty big.

The commercial sector has its poster children as well. Energy companies have amassed huge amounts of geophysical data. Pharmaceutical companies routinely munch their way through enormous amounts of drug testing data. Commercial sites, such as Facebook (*http://www.facebook.com*) and Twitter (*http://www.twitter.com*) maintain huge amounts of data that changes moment by moment, as well. Large organizations increasingly face the need to maintain large amounts of structured and unstructured data to comply with government regulations. Recent court cases have also lead them to keep masses of documents, email messages, and other forms of electronic communication that may be required if they face litigation.

The following virtualization technology is typically in use when people discuss "big data":

- Storage virtualization (distributed file systems)
- Virtual processing (parallel processing monitors, workload management monitors, memory virtualization)
- Management for virtual environments

If your organization is dealing with extremely large amounts of data or data that changes more rapidly than a typical database can manage, you are clearly in the big data category.

Since the requirements for "big data" applications differ from many other forms of structured data, many suppliers are offering new data management tools. Sometimes the suppliers call their products *NoSQL databases*. They may also talk about segmenting the database so that pieces of it may be spread over many machines. In this case, many suppliers speak about packaging and supporting open source data management technologies such as Apache's Hadoop and Cassandra projects.

Clusters

There are many different uses for a configuration that harnesses the power of many (up to thousands of) systems (see Figure 9-2). Although different technology may be in use, all of these configurations are called clusters. The fact that the same word is used to describe different uses of technology creates quite a bit of confusion. Depending upon the requirements, different virtualization technology may be in use.

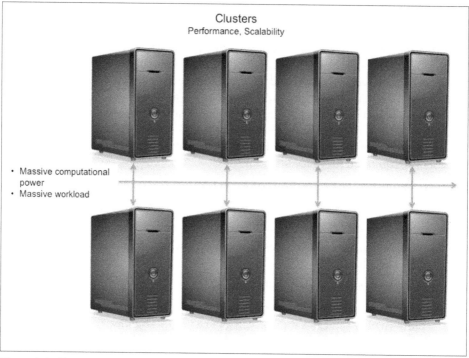

Figure 9-2. *Clusters*

Here are the typical requirements and technology:

High performance
> When huge amounts of computational power must be applied to speed up the processing of a single task, a parallel processing monitor, a form of processing virtualization, is used to harness the computational power of many systems. These clusters may include desktop systems as well as servers. This type of configuration is often used for modeling financial risk, nondestructive testing, rendering digital graphics, or other forms of modeling. Typically, these tasks run directly on the physical systems rather than being encapsulated into virtual machines or run in partitions when operating system virtualization is being used.

Scalability

When large numbers of people need to access the same application, a similar system configuration might be harnessed using workload management monitors, a form of virtual processing software. As transactions come in to be processed, the workload manager sends them to the system that has the most available capacity. Since performance is also a critical requirement in this use case, it is quite likely that the applications will be hosted directly on the physical systems, rather than being hosted on a virtual server. Server-centric application virtualization technology often contains a workload management function. Even though the workload management is happening at the application level, the multiserver configuration might be called a cluster.

Big data storage

Memory virtualization or distributed cache software is used to spread data out among a large number of systems, making it possible to access and update large amounts of data very quickly. Sometimes this configuration is described as a Hadoop or Cassandra cluster.

Storage cluster

In this case, storage servers, not general-purpose computing systems, are clustered together to create a very large high-performance storage environment for general-purpose computing functions. Distributed file system software might be used to access this data. The storage servers might use a special-purpose storage network called a SAN. Storage server suppliers also support a form of memory virtualization among the members of the storage server cluster.

Desktop Virtualization

Desktop virtualization is the use of several virtualization technologies, either together or separately. Let's look at each of these cases in turn.

When "desktop virtualization" is used to describe making it possible for people to access a physical or virtual system remotely, access virtualization technology is used to capture the user interface portion of an application. It is then converted to a neutral format and projected across the network to a device that can display the user interface and allow the user to enter and access information (see Figure 9-3). This means that just about any type of network-enabled device could be used to access the application. Suppliers such as Citrix, Microsoft, and VMware offer client software for tablets, smartphones, laptops, and PC, making it possible for users of those devices to access the applications running elsewhere on the network.

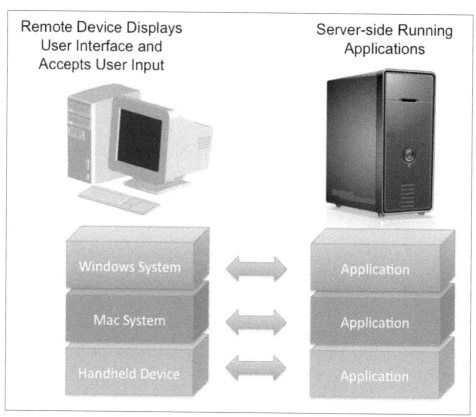

Figure 9-3. *Desktop virtualization via access virtualization*

When "desktop virtualization" is used to describe encapsulating an application using client-side application virtualization technology and then projecting it in whole or piecemeal to a remote system for execution, the application could either remain on that client device or be deleted once the user completes the task, depending on the settings used by the IT administrator (see Figure 9-4). This means, of course, that the client system has to run the operating system needed by the application. So, Windows applications, for example, would need to run on Windows executing on a PC or laptop.

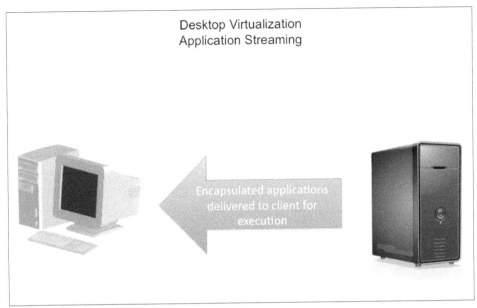

Desktop Virtualization
Application Streaming

Encapsulated applications delivered to client for execution

Figure 9-4. Desktop virtualization via application virtualization

When "desktop virtualization" is used to describe encapsulating the entire stack of software that runs on a client system, the phase starts to take on a great deal of complexity (see Figure 9-5). That encapsulated virtual client system becomes highly mobile. Here are the possibilities:

- One or more virtual client systems could execute on a single physical client system. This allows personal applications to run side by side with locked-down corporate applications.

- Local execution. Virtual client systems could run on a local blade server. The user interface is projected to physical PCs, laptops, or thin client systems using access virtualization technology.

- Remote execution. Virtual client systems could run on a server that resides in the organization's data center. The user interface is projected to physical PCs, laptops, or thin client systems using access virtualization technology.

Since the industry is using the same phrase to describe all of these different approaches, the concept of desktop virtualization can be quite confusing to those unfamiliar with all of the different types of technology that could be pressed into service.

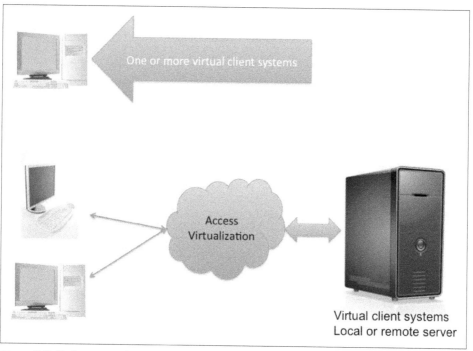

Figure 9-5. Desktop virtualization via processing virtualization

High-Performance Computing

When an application or a workload require more computational power than is available from a single computer because of either technical or financial limitations, organizations harness a large number of computers (yes, a cluster) to work on a single task or a small number of tasks (see Figure 9-6). Typically a parallel processing monitor, a type of processing virtualization software, is used to manage these systems. The monitor sends some work to each system. As systems complete their tasks, they send the results back to the system running the monitor and request another task.

This approach is used to support financial modeling, geophysical modeling, risk analysis, scientific research, digital content creation, and a number of other tasks that require enormous processing power.

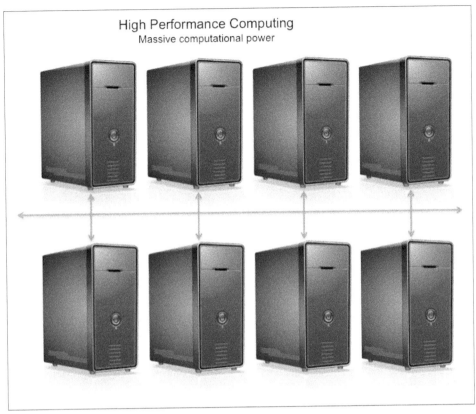

High Performance Computing
Massive computational power

Figure 9-6. High-performance computing

Server Virtualization

Server virtualization is the use of either virtual machine technology or operating system virtualization and partitioning technology to make a single physical server support multiple independent workloads (see Figure 9-7). If operating system virtualization and partitioning technology is used, all of the workloads must be supported by a single operating system. If virtual machine technology is being used, each virtual machine runs a different operating system. This could be different versions of the same operating system (such as Windows 2003, Windows 2008, etc.) or many different operating systems (Windows, Linux, UNIX, etc.).

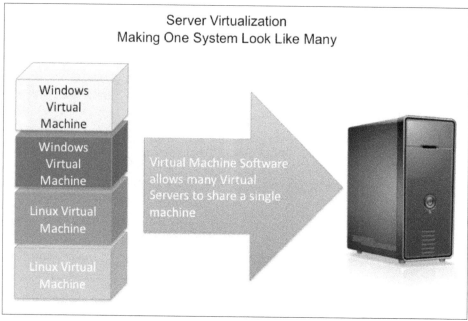

Figure 9-7. Server virtualization

This approach more fully utilizes the power of the underlying physical system. Since all of the individual workloads are sharing a single computer, this approach is not selected when the goal is high-performance computing or extreme transaction processing.

Extreme Transaction Processing

Extreme transaction processing (see Figure 9-8) is the use of a number of virtualization technologies—such as workload managers, memory virtualization, and virtual storage technology—to create an environment that can support hundreds of thousands or, perhaps, millions of transactions per second. The work is spread over a large number of computing and storage resources (yes, another version of a cluster).

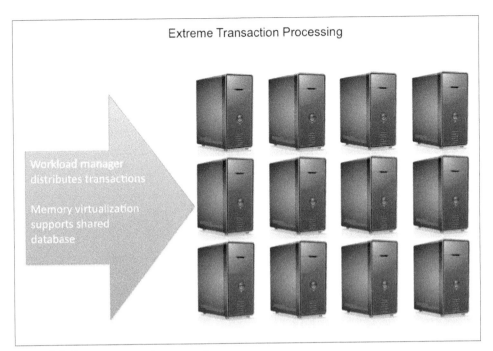

Figure 9-8. Extreme transaction processing

CHAPTER 10

Summary

Virtualization Is a Double-Edged Sword

As with many types of technology, virtualization is a very powerful tool. If it is used properly, organizations gain quite a number of benefits:

- Applications can perform faster than today's processor technology would normally support or make it possible to use many lower-cost, lower-performance machines to handle work that would normally be assigned to a larger, more expensive machine.
- Applications can scale to support more users than would be possible on a single system.
- Application environments can be much more reliable and dependable. System configurations can be constructed that will survive the loss of any single component.
- Client applications can be isolated from one another so that previously incompatible applications can share the same machine.
- Personal workloads and locked-down corporate workloads can share the same machine.
- Server use can be optimized.

Virtualization, however, is not a panacea. Using the wrong tool or using the right tool improperly can result in poor performance, higher costs for the organization, and the organization not being able to meet its objectives.

Virtualization is best used when the organization has an overarching plan and is developing solutions to fit an architecture rather than focusing on the "hot" tool of the moment.

Where to Go Next

Before embarking on the journey to a more virtualized environment, an organization should answer the following questions:

- What are the organization's goals?
- What needs to be done to achieve those goals?
- Who needs to be involved to marshal all of the necessary resources?
- What types of technology are needed to build the tools that will help the organization achieve its goals?
- Does the plan allows for technological improvements, new technology, or changes in suppliers?

In short, the organization needs to have a plan, needs to implement solutions according to that plan, and needs to carefully monitor ongoing development and operations to make sure the organization achieves its goals.

As Yogi Berra once said, "If you don't know where you're going, you might end up somewhere else."

If your organization doesn't have the appropriate expertise on staff, it would be very wise to seek out a supplier or consultants to help.

About the Author

Daniel Kusnetzky, distinguished analyst and founder of the Kusnetzky Group LLC, has been involved with information technology since the late 1970s. He's interested in system software, virtualization technology, cloud computing, and mobility.

Colophon

The animal on the cover of *Virtualization: A Manager's Guide* is a condor.

The cover image is from *Wood's Animate Creations*. The cover font is Adobe ITC Garamond. The text font is Linotype Birka; the heading font is Adobe Myriad Condensed; and the code font is LucasFont's TheSansMonoCondensed.

Get even more for your money.

Join the O'Reilly Community, and register the O'Reilly books you own. It's free, and you'll get:

- $4.99 ebook upgrade offer
- 40% upgrade offer on O'Reilly print books
- Membership discounts on books and events
- Free lifetime updates to ebooks and videos
- Multiple ebook formats, DRM FREE
- Participation in the O'Reilly community
- Newsletters
- Account management
- 100% Satisfaction Guarantee

Signing up is easy:

1. **Go to: oreilly.com/go/register**
2. **Create an O'Reilly login.**
3. **Provide your address.**
4. **Register your books.**

Note: English-language books only

To order books online:
oreilly.com/store

For questions about products or an order:
orders@oreilly.com

To sign up to get topic-specific email announcements and/or news about upcoming books, conferences, special offers, and new technologies:
elists@oreilly.com

For technical questions about book content:
booktech@oreilly.com

To submit new book proposals to our editors:
proposals@oreilly.com

O'Reilly books are available in multiple DRM-free ebook formats. For more information:
oreilly.com/ebooks

Spreading the knowledge of innovators   oreilly.com

The information you need, when and where you need it.

With Safari Books Online, you can:

Access the contents of thousands of technology and business books

- Quickly search over 7000 books and certification guides
- Download whole books or chapters in PDF format, at no extra cost, to print or read on the go
- Copy and paste code
- Save up to 35% on O'Reilly print books
- **New!** Access mobile-friendly books directly from cell phones and mobile devices

Stay up-to-date on emerging topics before the books are published

- Get on-demand access to evolving manuscripts.
- Interact directly with authors of upcoming books

Explore thousands of hours of video on technology and design topics

- Learn from expert video tutorials
- Watch and replay recorded conference sessions